# Anne of Green Gables
## Reading Booklet

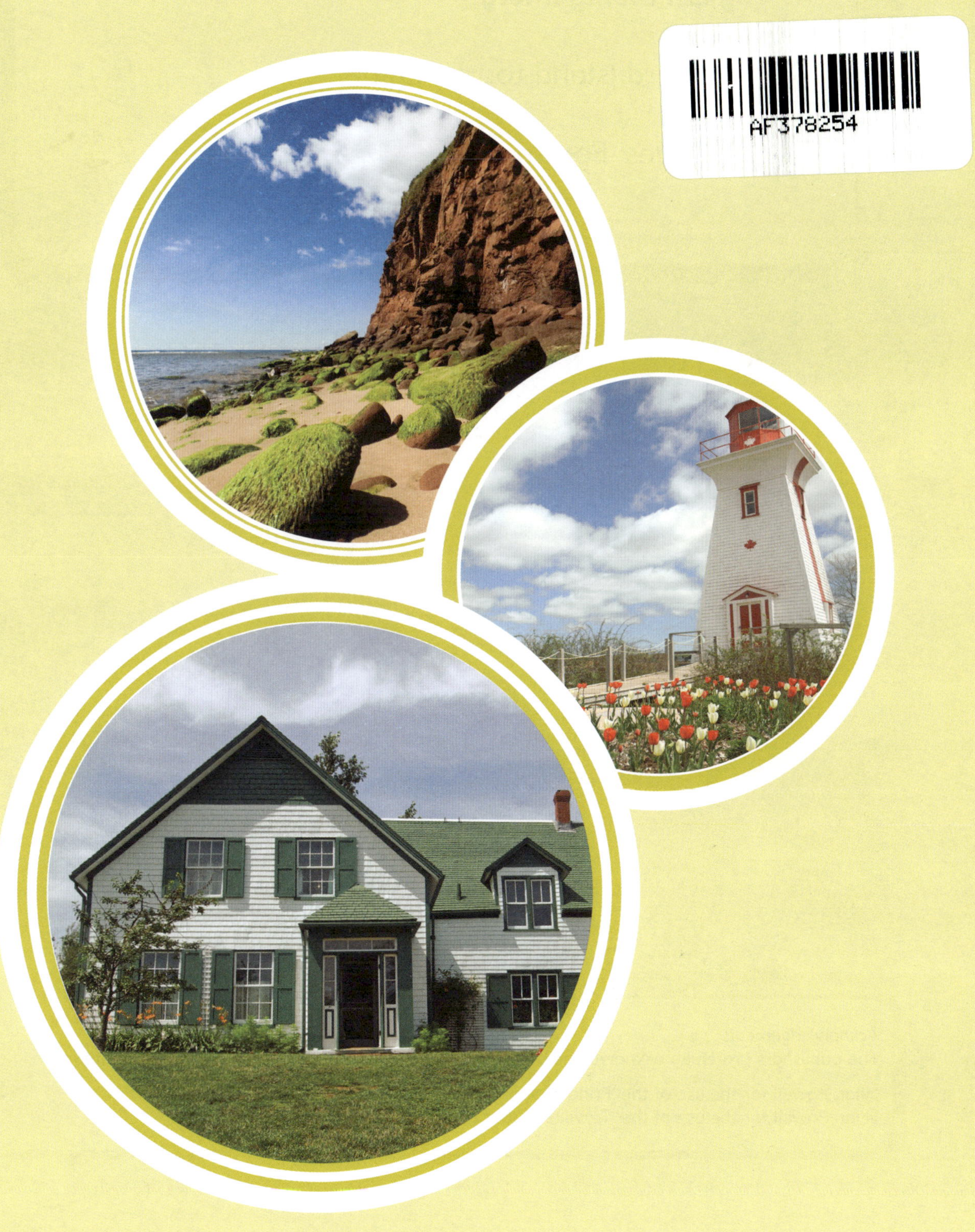

# Contents




*Acknowledgements*

The publishers gratefully acknowledge permission to reproduce the following copyright material:

Jillian Powell for the use of the 'Prince Edward Island tourist guide'. Text © 2013, Jillian Powell.
Jillian Powell for the use of the 'Traveller Tales: Forum'. Text © 2013, Jillian Powell.

# Anne of Green Gables
### by LM Montgomery

Matthew Cuthbert is an elderly farmer who has lived all of his life in Prince Edward Island, with his sister Marilla. He has taken his horse and cart to the station to collect an orphan boy to help him with farm work, only to find a young girl has been sent to him. He decides to take her home to see what Marilla thinks…

She came out of her reverie with a deep sigh and looked at him with the dreamy gaze of a soul that had been wondering afar, star-led.

"Oh, Mr. Cuthbert," she whispered, "that place we came through—that white place—what was it?"

"Well now, you must mean the Avenue," said Matthew after a few moments' profound reflection. "It is a kind of pretty place."

"Pretty? Oh, PRETTY doesn't seem the right word to use. Nor beautiful, either. They don't go far enough. Oh, it was wonderful— wonderful. It's the first thing I ever saw that couldn't be improved upon by imagination. It just satisfies me here"—she put one hand on her breast—"it made a queer funny ache and yet it was a pleasant ache. Did you ever have an ache like that, Mr. Cuthbert?"

"Well now, I just can't recollect that I ever had."

"I have it lots of time—whenever I see anything royally beautiful. But they shouldn't call that lovely place the Avenue. There is no meaning in a name like that. They should call it—let me see—the White Way of Delight. Isn't that a nice imaginative name? When I don't like the name of a place or a person I always imagine a new one and always think of them so. There was a girl at the asylum whose name was Hepzibah Jenkins, but I always imagined her as Rosalia DeVere. Other people may call that place the Avenue, but I shall always call it the White Way of Delight. Have we really only another mile to go before we get home? I'm glad and I'm sorry. I'm sorry because this drive has been so pleasant and I'm always sorry when pleasant things end. Something still pleasanter may come after, but you can never be sure. And it's so often the case that it isn't pleasanter. That has been my experience anyhow. But I'm glad to think of getting home. You see, I've never had a real home since I can remember. It gives me that pleasant ache again just to think of coming to a really truly home. Oh, isn't that pretty!"

They had driven over the crest of a hill. Below them was a pond, looking almost like a river so long and winding was it. A bridge spanned it midway and from there to its lower end, where an amber-hued belt of sand-hills shut it in from the dark blue gulf beyond, the water was a glory of many shifting hues—the most spiritual shadings of crocus and rose and ethereal green, with other elusive tintings for which no name has ever been found. Above the bridge the pond ran up into fringing groves of fir and maple and lay all darkly translucent in their wavering shadows. Here and there a wild plum leaned out from the bank like a white-clad girl tip-toeing to her own reflection. From the marsh at the head of the pond came the clear, mournfully-sweet chorus of the frogs. There was a little gray house peering around a white apple orchard on a slope beyond and, although it was not yet quite dark, a light was shining from one of its windows.

"That's Barry's pond," said Matthew.

"Oh, I don't like that name, either. I shall call it—let me see—the Lake of Shining Waters. Yes, that is the right name for it. I know because of the thrill. When I hit on a name that suits exactly it gives me a thrill. Do things ever give you a thrill?"

Matthew ruminated.

"Well now, yes. It always kind of gives me a thrill to see them ugly white grubs that spade up in the cucumber beds. I hate the look of them."

"Oh, I don't think that can be exactly the same kind of a thrill. Do you think it can! There doesn't seem to be much connection between grubs and lakes of shining waters, does there! But why do other people call it Barry's pond?"

## Paper 1: Anne of Green Gables

# Prince Edward Island tourist guide

### Welcome to Prince Edward Island, home of *Anne of Green Gables*

A warm welcome awaits you on Prince Edward Island, also known as the 'Gentle Island' or PEI. The smallest province in Canada, this island in the Gulf of Lawrence has the warmest beaches north of the Carolinas. Here you can explore over 2000 sq miles (5600 sq kilometres) of enchanting pastoral landscape, as well as the famous red sandy beaches and fine golf courses. The island is considered a paradise by visitors who enjoy the great outdoors, offering every kind of activity from beachcombing and seal watching to snorkelling and parasailing. Cycling is a great way to get around. Rent a bicycle from one of the many hire shops and explore many pleasant trails, including the Confederation Trail which stretches for 292 miles (470 kilometres).

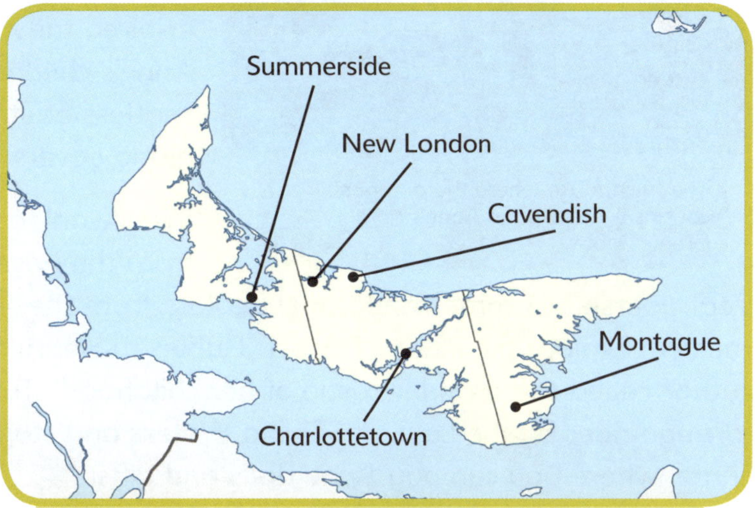


The long coastline is rich in bays and inlets, making it ideal for sports including fishing and kayaking

There's plenty for children too. Safe, sandy beaches and fun-packed amusement parks, and the kids will love our award-winning Cows ice cream.

When you've worked up an appetite why not sample some of the island's renowned fresh shellfish, including lobsters, oysters and Island Gold blue mussels and visit a mussel farm to see how they grow.

## Paper 1: Anne of Green Gables

The farmhouse where the author's cousins lived inspired Anne's home, Green Gables

PEI is the birthplace of LM Montgomery, author of the much-loved children's classic *Anne of Green Gables*. You will find a wealth of visitor attractions in Cavendish. Visit Green Gables Heritage Place, the farmhouse that inspired the novel's setting. Look around Anne's childhood bedroom and Marilla's spotless pantry, then take a relaxing walk along Lovers' Lane into the Haunted Woods.

Visit Avonlea village and chat with characters from the novels; pet barnyard animals and treat yourself to some candy or chocolate from the Anne of Green Gables Chocolate Factory. Explore the Anne of Green Gables museum at Park Corner, in the house the author called the 'wonder castle of her childhood'. Take one of Matthew's delightful carriage rides by the Lake of Shining Waters and stop off at the gift shop of the same name, where you can buy Anne dolls and gifts.

If you are visiting in the summer, don't forget to book seats in advance for *Anne of Green Gables – The Musical*, at the Confederation Arts Centre in the capital city Charlottetown, which hosts the annual LM Montgomery Festival.

### Biography: LM Montgomery

Lucy Maud Montgomery was born in a house overlooking New London Harbour on Prince Edward Island in 1874. After her mother died when she was a baby, she lived with her grandparents who ran the Cavendish Post Office. When Maud (as she was known) left school she trained as a teacher, but she had already begun writing poems and short stories for local newspapers and magazines. *Anne of Green Gables*, the novel that made her famous, was published in 1908 and was followed by several sequels. Set in the 1870s, it tells the story of Anne Shirley, a feisty red-haired orphan taken in by kindly brother and sister, Matthew and Marilla Cuthbert who had been intending to adopt a young boy to help them on their farm. The setting was inspired by the green-gabled farmhouse that Maud often visited as a child, where her cousins the Macneills lived. Read by millions around the world, the novel has been translated into 36 languages and inspired stage, television and film adaptations. The author married in 1911 and had three children. She died in 1942 and was buried at Cavendish on Prince Edward Island.

LM Montgomery when she was in her twenties

## Paper 1: Anne of Green Gables

# Traveller Tales: Forum

**8 replies**     **PEI - Not what it once was**     Expand view »

---

**bettyB**    #1

I have just returned to Prince Edward Island for the first time in thirty years. But what has happened to this lovely island? It has become a theme park. Cavendish is awash with tacky souvenir shops and restaurants cashing in on the Anne of Green Gables name. Why must tourism be allowed to spoil what was once a peaceful getaway?

*Join date: May 2012*
*Posts: 47*

*Posted yesterday, 08:59 AM*    **Reply**

---

**islandJo**    #2

I've lived on PEI all my life and believe me to us islanders it is still a lovely place of natural beauty and not a theme park! True, Cavendish has been developed to bring in the tourists, but islanders need jobs and tourism (along with farming and fishing) is one of our main industries. BettyB, you complain about tourism, but you are a tourist after all!

*Join date: Dec 2010*
*Posts: 82*

*Posted yesterday, 10:37 AM*    **Reply**

---

**bettyB**    #3

The problem is not tourism! PEI is always going to attract visitors because it has spectacular natural scenery, sandy beaches and warm waters. What I object to is gross commercialisation. The enchanting world that LM Montgomery captured is far from the fantasyland that now engulfs parts of the north shore, with its strip malls, motels, amusement parks and ferris wheels!

*Join date: May 2012*
*Posts: 48*

*Posted yesterday, 10:48 PM*    **Reply**

---

**danielr**    #4

As a young person growing up on PEI I agree with islandJo. Unemployment here is above the national average and without the tourist industry many young people would not be able to stay on the island. I have just got a job at the Shining Waters – Ingleside resort and I have friends who are working at campsites or in restaurants which all rely on tourism. Yes, it's a bit tacky, but we all have to live.

*Join date: Jan 2013*
*Posts: 12*

*Posted yesterday, 12:05 PM*    **Reply**

---

## Paper 1: Anne of Green Gables

**shannon61** #5

Join date: Aug 2011
Posts: 23

My family used to vacation every year on PEI because we love the outdoor life and the island has much to offer for those who enjoy cycling and other sports. But I agree with bettyB. Cavendish has become like a stage set, with 'animators' dressed up in character and endless shops selling straw hats with sewn-on braids and Anne dolls. It all cheapens LM Montgomery's legacy.

Posted yesterday, 3:19 PM    **Reply**

**familyMorris** #6

Join date: May 2009
Posts: 34

I visited the island with my family for the first time last year and we loved it! I read all the Anne books when I was growing up and have now passed them on to my daughter. She loved all the Anne souvenirs and we had great fun dressing up and getting our photo taken. There are so many fun activities for families in Avonlea village that even when it is raining (as it was when we were there) there is still plenty to do and enjoy. We will certainly return!

Posted today, 3:42 PM    **Reply**

**DJ3000** #7

Join date: Feb 2012
Posts: 18

I just finished reading *Anne of Green Gables* – it was wonderful! Are there other books by LM Montgomery? Prince Edward Island is such a perfect setting for her stories.

Posted today, 4:07 PM    **Reply**

**familyMorris** #8

Join date: May 2009
Posts: 35

Hi DJ. There's a whole series of AGG books! Have you tried *Anne of Avonlea*?

Posted today, 5:32 PM    **Reply**

# READING TEST

## PAPER 1: ANNE OF GREEN GABLES

**LEVEL 6
PRACTICE PAPERS**

| | |
|---|---|
| First name | |
| Middle name | |
| Last name | |
| Date of birth | Day          Month          Year |
| Year group | |
| School | |

## REMEMBER

- This paper is 60 minutes long.
- You have 10 minutes to read the reading booklets before answering the questions. During this time you should not open your answer booklet.
- You then have 50 minutes to write your answers in this booklet.
- There are 17 questions totalling 32 marks.

# Paper 1: Anne of Green Gables



Questions 1–6 are about *Anne of Green Gables* on pages **3–4** in the Reading Booklet.

**1.** The extract begins:

*She came out of her reverie with a deep sigh and looked at him with the dreamy gaze of a soul that had been wondering afar, star-led.*

Explain what the author is trying to tell us about the lead character in this sentence.

_______________________________________________

_______________________________________________

_______________________________________________

_______________________________________________

_______________________________________________

_______________________________________________

_______________________________________________

_______________________________________________

_______________________________________________

3

# Paper 1: Anne of Green Gables

| | Marks |
|---|---|

**2.** What do you discover about Anne's past? Support your answer by referring to paragraph 6.

1

**3.** Find a quote that best illustrates Anne's optimistic outlook on life. Refer to paragraphs 1–6 in your answer.

1

# Paper 1: Anne of Green Gables

**4.** Look at paragraph 4, beginning *"Pretty?..."*

How does the author convey Anne's excitement?

_______________________________________________

_______________________________________________

_______________________________________________

_______________________________________________

_______________________________________________

Marks

2

# Paper 1: Anne of Green Gables

**5.** Decide on a single word each that best defines each character and find a quote to illustrate your choice of word.

**a) Anne**

Defining word: _______________________

Quote: _______________________

_______________________

_______________________

_______________________

**b) Matthew**

Defining word: _______________________

Quote: _______________________

_______________________

_______________________

_______________________



2

## Paper 1: Anne of Green Gables

**6.** Explain what the author's choice of language achieves in paragraph 7.

Marks

______________________________________________

______________________________________________

______________________________________________

______________________________________________

______________________________________________

______________________________________________

______________________________________________

______________________________________________

3

## Paper 1: Anne of Green Gables



Questions 7–11 are about *The Prince Edward Island tourist guide* on pages **5–6** in the Reading Booklet.

**7.** How do the opening paragraphs of the Tourist Brochure encourage us to keep reading?

_________________________________________________

_________________________________________________

_________________________________________________

_________________________________________________

_________________________________________________

_________________________________________________

_________________________________________________

2

**8.** Find two words or expressions that suggest that the Island has a good reputation with tourists.

- _________________________________________________

- _________________________________________________

1

# Paper 1: Anne of Green Gables

**9.** What might lead you to think that LM Montgomery based *Anne of Green Gables* on her own childhood? Refer to the biography section in your answer.

Marks

2

**10.** How does the brochure try to make Anne of Green Gables feel real? Support your answer by referring to the text.

2

# Paper 1: Anne of Green Gables

**11.** Do you think the brochure is presented effectively? Give reasons for your answer and refer to the text.

Marks

2

## Paper 1: Anne of Green Gables

> Questions 12–16 are about the *Traveller Tales: Forum* on page **7** in the Reading Booklet.



**12.** Tick which of these quotes is a fact rather than an opinion.

| | | |
|---|---|---|
| **bettyB** | *...PEI is always going to attract visitors because it has spectacular natural scenery...* | |
| **islandJo** | *...to us islanders it is still a lovely place of natural beauty and not a theme park...* | |
| **danielr** | *...Yes, it's a bit tacky...* | |
| **shannon61** | *...Cavendish has become like a stage set...* | |
| **familyMorris** | *...even when it is raining (as it was when we were there) there is still plenty to do...* | |

1

**13.** Find two words that **bettyB** uses to exaggerate her opinions in her entries.

- ______________________________________________

- ______________________________________________

1

## Paper 1: Anne of Green Gables

**14.** Explain what **familyMorris** and **shannon61**'s entries tell us about their views.

**shannon61** ______________________________

______________________________

______________________________

______________________________

**familyMorris** ______________________________

______________________________

______________________________

Marks

**2**

**15.** Look at the contribution from **danielr**. How does he try and get his point across?

______________________________

______________________________

______________________________

**2**

**16.** Would the web-based discussion help someone who has never been to Prince Edward Island to form their own views? Is it more helpful than a face-to-face discussion?



2

## Paper 1: Anne of Green Gables

Marks

Question 17 is about *Anne of Green Gables* and *The Prince Edward Island Tourist Guide* in the Reading Booklet.

**17.** How do the book extract and travel brochure present their views of Prince Edward Island? How are they the same? How are they different?

_______________________________________________

_______________________________________________

_______________________________________________

_______________________________________________

_______________________________________________

_______________________________________________

_______________________________________________

_______________________________________________

_______________________________________________

_______________________________________________

3

**End of test**

[BLANK PAGE]

[BLANK PAGE]

# Marks

| Question | Focus | Possible marks | Actual marks |
| --- | --- | --- | --- |
| 1 | AF5 | 3 | |
| 2 | AF2 | 1 | |
| 3 | AF3 | 1 | |
| 4 | AF5 | 2 | |
| 5 | AF3 | 2 | |
| 6 | AF5 | 3 | |
| 7 | AF4 | 2 | |
| 8 | AF2 | 1 | |
| 9 | AF3 | 2 | |
| 10 | AF5 | 2 | |
| 11 | AF4 | 2 | |
| 12 | AF2 | 1 | |
| 13 | AF3 | 1 | |
| 14 | AF6 | 2 | |
| 15 | AF4 | 2 | |
| 16 | AF7 | 2 | |
| 17 | AF7 | 3 | |
| **Total** | | **32** | |

$$\text{Percentage mark} = \frac{\text{child score}}{32} \times 100 = \underline{\hspace{3cm}} \%$$

SCHOLASTIC

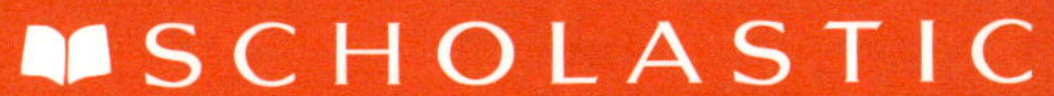

# Animal Power
## Reading Booklet

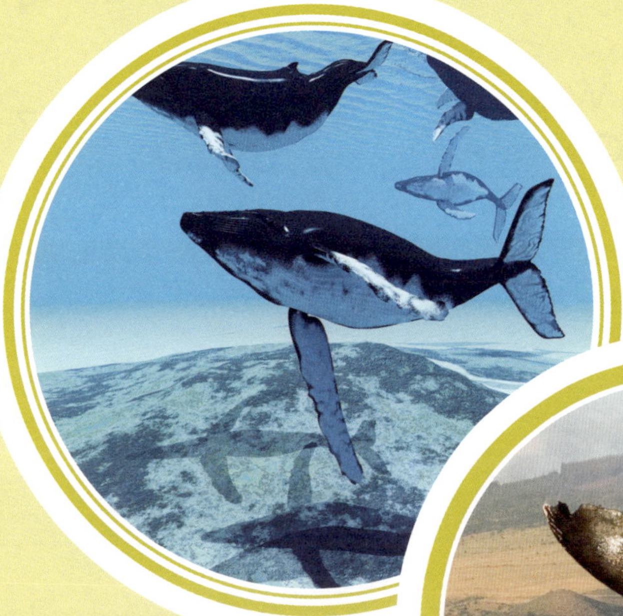

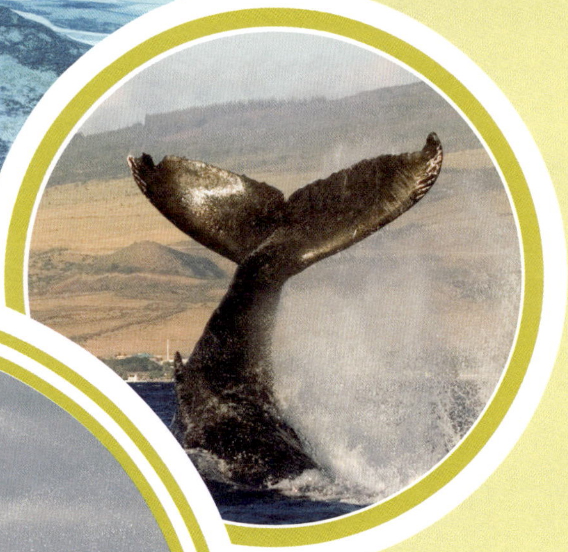

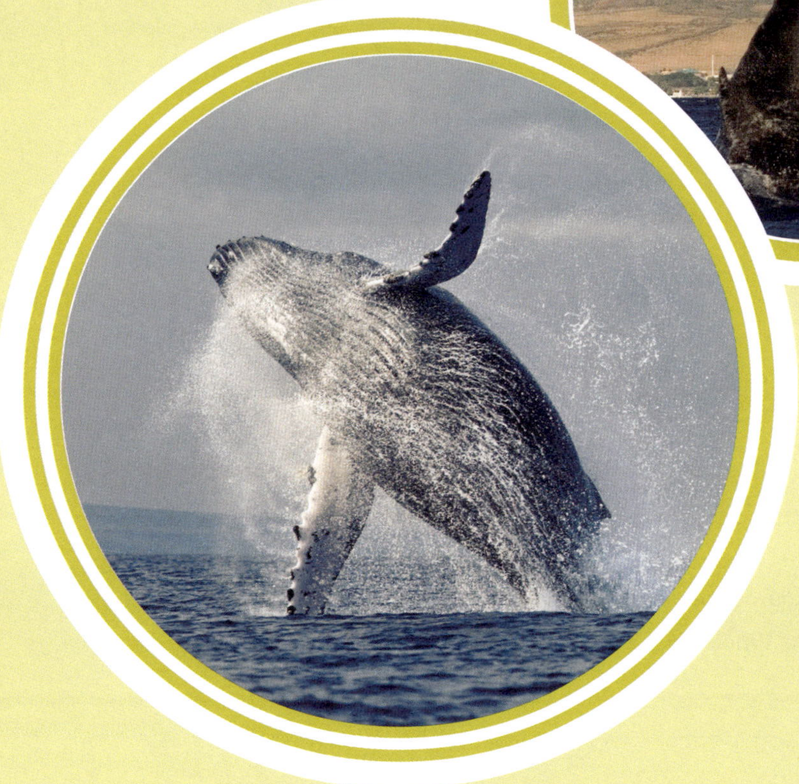

# Contents




**Acknowledgements**
The publishers gratefully acknowledge permission to reproduce the following copyright material:

Eileen Jones for the use of the 'Whales fact file' by Eileen Jones. Text © 2013, Eileen Jones.

# The Tyger By William Blake

William Blake wrote this poem over 200 years ago when most tigers lived in the wild in countries far away, not in zoos. This was long before photography and video were invented, and few English people would have ever seen one, although they may have heard about them.

Tyger Tyger, burning bright,
In the forests of the night;
What immortal hand or eye,
Could frame thy fearful symmetry?

In what distant deeps or skies.
Burnt the fire of thine eyes?
On what wings dare he aspire?
What the hand, dare seize the fire?

And what shoulder, & what art,
Could twist the sinews of thy heart?
And when thy heart began to beat,
What dread hand? & what dread feet?

What the hammer? what the chain,
In what furnace was thy brain?
What the anvil? what dread grasp,
Dare its deadly terrors clasp!

When the stars threw down their spears
And water'd heaven with their tears:
Did he smile his work to see?
Did he who made the Lamb make thee?

Tyger Tyger burning bright,
In the forests of the night:
What immortal hand or eye,
Dare frame thy fearful symmetry?

## Paper 2: Animal power

# Whales fact file

If you're interested in animals you will love learning about whales: they are unique and extraordinary creatures, and we have more in common with them than you might imagine...

### Types

Whales, like us, are mammals. They number around 80 different species, and belong to the animal order *cetecea*, which can be further divided into *baleen* whales and *toothed* whales. Toothed whales outnumber baleens in species. Their teeth are for grabbing and chewing prey, attack and defence, or exhibiting dominance. Cooperating in groups or pods, they hunt, migrate and rear young together. Baleen whales are usually superior in size, with two

blowholes rather than one and a baleen palate instead of teeth. They swim with their mouths agape, filter feeding by expelling the water through their gills and retaining food inside their baleen bristles. Their annual migration to warm-water breeding grounds often requires long journeys from cold-water feeding grounds.

| How are whales like other mammals? | How are whales special? |
| --- | --- |
| They use lungs to breathe air. | A layer of blubber lies under their skin. |
| They are warm-blooded. | They breathe through a blowhole on their head. |
| They produce milk to feed their young. | Their bodies have the streamlined form of a fish. |
| They have some hair. | They have paddle-shaped forelimbs or flippers. |

### Habitat and diet

Whales can be found in oceans throughout the world, usually dictated by their species. Their diets very much depend on their environments, ranging from microscopic plankton (eaten in vast quantities) to large marine animals.

## Behaviour

Whales are usually quite active in the water. Most whales *breach* out of the water and some slap their tails on the surface, perhaps to warn one another of local danger. They communicate through loud, singing sounds, sometimes audible miles away. Travel may be solitary or in pods during annual migration to breeding grounds.

## Threats

The growth of the whaling industry over the last few centuries saw whales hunted for oil and food, leaving many species such as Blue Whales endangered. The negative depiction of the ferocious fictional whale, *Moby Dick*, encouraged human antipathy.

Modern reforms and changed public attitudes have ended the whaling industry in most countries, but nevertheless some countries still continue their annual whale hunts. Further threats come from beaching; contaminated and polluted waters; and reduced populations of krill due to climate change raising temperatures in the Antarctic Ocean. (Krill is a small crustacean, the main food source for some whale species.)

| | |
|---|---|
| **Breaching** | Whales sometimes leap out of the water, slapping the water loudly when coming down. Breaching may be for play, to loosen skin parasites or for communication. |
| **Echolocation** | Whales use sound to help them navigate and find things, usually high-pitched clicks that bounce off objects. The returning echo lets them gauge proximity, shape, size and texture. |
| **Beaching** | Whales sometimes come on to land, and can die if they become beached. They can beach in large numbers. No one quite knows why, though it is thought that their hearing has become damaged or confused. |
| **Blubber** | Blubber is an ingenious layer of insulating fat. It keeps the whale's temperature stable, stores food energy, and helps it to stay afloat; it ranges from 5cm thick (grey whales) to 30cm thick (blue whales). |

## Paper 2: Animal power

# Well-known whales

| Species | Average size | Appearance | Behaviour | Interesting facts |
| --- | --- | --- | --- | --- |
| Beluga | 18m | White, with a stout body and short, rounded and wide flippers. | Regular songs and chatter give the nickname 'sea canary'. | Beluga means 'white one' in Russian. |
| Bowhead | 19m | A large bow-shaped head makes up to 40% of its body length. | Uses songs to locate large masses of krill and to communicate. | Small eyes and huge lips. |
| Grey | 15m | Grey with white spots. | Hairy bristles (vibrissae) on the snout and front of head act as sensors. | Whalers used to call them 'devilfish' because of their fierceness. |
| Humpback | 13m | Raises and bends its back for a dive, accentuating the hump. | Males sing the loudest and most complicated song of any animal. | Slow swimmers, so tourist and whaler boats can often get near. |
| Blue | 34m | Grey at surface; luminous blue when seen underwater. | Emits very loud, low-frequency whistles, louder than a jet engine. | Largest animal to have ever lived. |
| Sperm | 16m | Has a large head to contain a huge brain weighing about 9kg. | Travel in pods and form strong, long-lasting bonds with other members. | The deepest diving whale. |
| Right | 17m | Has a large bulbous head. | Swim quite slowly. Mother and calf form a long-term bond. | Named the 'right' whale to kill due to ample blubber, oil and bone. |
| Narwhal | 5m (not including tusk) | Has two teeth in the upper jaw; the left one is a tusk and projects from the jaw for 2–3m. | The tusk is used as a jousting weapon to establish dominance when finding a mate. | In medieval times, they believed narwhal tusks that washed ashore were from unicorns. |

# The Wind in the Willows

by Kenneth Grahame, 1908

It was a bright morning in the early part of summer; the river had resumed its wonted banks and its accustomed pace, and a hot sun seemed to be pulling everything green and bushy and spiky up out of the earth towards him, as if by strings. The Mole and the Water Rat had been up since dawn, very busy on matters connected with boats and the opening of the boating season; painting and varnishing, mending paddles, repairing cushions, hunting for missing boat-hooks, and so on; and were finishing breakfast in their little parlour and eagerly discussing their plans for the day, when a heavy knock sounded at the door.

"Bother!" said the Rat, all over egg. "See who it is, Mole, like a good chap, since you've finished."

The Mole went to attend the summons, and the Rat heard him utter a cry of surprise. Then he flung the parlour door open, and announced with much importance, "Mr. Badger!"

This was a wonderful thing, indeed, that the Badger should pay a formal call on them, or indeed on anybody. He generally had to be caught, if you wanted him badly, as he slipped quietly along a hedgerow of an early morning or a late evening, or else hunted up in his own house in the middle of the Wood, which was a serious undertaking.

The Badger strode heavily into the room, and stood looking at the two animals with an expression full of seriousness. The Rat let his egg-spoon fall on the table-cloth, and sat open-mouthed.

"The hour has come!" said the Badger at last with great solemnity.

"What hour?" asked the Rat uneasily, glancing at the clock on the mantelpiece.

"WHOSE hour, you should rather say," replied the Badger. "Why, Toad's hour! The hour of Toad! I said I would take him in hand as soon as the winter was well over, and I'm going to take him in hand to-day!"

"Toad's hour, of course!" cried the Mole delightedly. "Hooray! I remember now! WE'LL teach him to be a sensible Toad!"

"This very morning," continued the Badger, taking an arm-chair, "as I learnt last night from a trustworthy source, another new and exceptionally powerful motor-car will arrive at Toad Hall on approval or return. At this very moment, perhaps, Toad is busy arraying himself in those singularly hideous habiliments so dear to him, which transform him from a (comparatively) good-looking Toad into an Object which throws any decent-minded animal that comes across it into a violent fit. We must be up and doing, ere it is too late. You two animals will accompany me instantly to Toad Hall, and the work of rescue shall be accomplished."

"Right you are!" cried the Rat, starting up. "We'll rescue the poor unhappy animal! We'll convert him! He'll be the most converted Toad that ever was before we've done with him!"

They set off up the road on their mission of mercy, Badger leading the way. Animals when in company walk in a proper and sensible manner, in single file, instead of sprawling all across the road and being of no use or support to each other in case of sudden trouble or danger.

They reached the carriage-drive of Toad Hall to find, as the Badger had anticipated, a shiny new motor-car, of great size, painted a bright red (Toad's favourite colour), standing in front of the house. As they neared the door it was flung open, and Mr. Toad, arrayed in goggles, cap, gaiters, and enormous overcoat, came swaggering down the steps, drawing on his gauntleted gloves.

"Hullo! Come on, you fellows!" he cried cheerfully on catching sight of them. "You're just in time to come with me for a jolly—to come for a jolly—for a—er—jolly——"

His hearty accents faltered and fell away as he noticed the stern unbending look on the countenances of his silent friends, and his invitation remained unfinished.

The Badger strode up the steps. "Take him inside," he said sternly to his companions. Then, as Toad was hustled through the door, struggling and protesting, he turned to the chauffeur in charge of the new motor-car.

"I'm afraid you won't be wanted to-day," he said. "Mr. Toad has changed his mind. He will not require the car. Please understand that this is final. You needn't wait." Then he followed the others inside and shut the door.

"Now then!" he said to the Toad, when the four of them stood together in the Hall, "first of all, take those ridiculous things off!"

"Shan't!" replied Toad, with great spirit. "What is the meaning of this gross outrage? I demand an instant explanation."

"Take them off him, then, you two," ordered the Badger briefly.

They had to lay Toad out on the floor, kicking and calling all sorts of names, before they could get to work properly. Then the Rat sat on him, and the Mole got his motor-clothes off him bit by bit, and they stood him up on his legs again. A good deal of his blustering spirit seemed to have evaporated with the removal of his fine panoply. Now that he was merely Toad, and no longer the Terror of the Highway, he giggled feebly and looked from one to the other appealingly, seeming quite to understand the situation.

# READING TEST

## PAPER 2: ANIMAL POWER

| | |
|---|---|
| First name | |
| Middle name | |
| Last name | |
| Date of birth | Day      Month      Year |
| Year group | |
| School | |

## REMEMBER

- This paper is 60 minutes long.
- You have 10 minutes to read the reading booklets before answering the questions. During this time you should not open your answer booklet.
- You then have 50 minutes to write your answers in this booklet.
- There are 17 questions totalling 32 marks.

## Paper 2: Animal power

Questions 1–4 are about 'The Tyger', on page **3** of the Reading Booklet.

**Marks**

**1.** Look at verse 1, what words suggest that the poet is referring to God?

1

**2.** *What the hammer? what the chain,*

   *In what furnace was thy brain?*

   (Verse 4)

Hammers, chains and furnaces are the equipment of blacksmiths. What makes this an effective metaphor?

3

**Paper 2: Animal power**



**3.** The poem contains lots of questions. Explain what these suggest about the poet's thoughts.

_______________________________________________

_______________________________________________

_______________________________________________

_______________________________________________

_______________________________________________

2

**4.** Why is starting and finishing the poem with almost the same verse effective?

_______________________________________________

_______________________________________________

_______________________________________________

_______________________________________________

2

## Paper 2: Animal power

Questions 5–11 are about the *Whales fact file* on pages **4–6** in the Reading Booklet.

**5.** What is the purpose of the opening paragraph of the fact file?

**6.** Identify two differences between baleen and toothed whales.

Marks

1

1

## Paper 2: Animal power

**7.** Why are habitat and diet discussed under a single heading and not two separate ones?

_______________________________________________

_______________________________________________

**8.** How does the chart on page 6 try to maintain your interest?

_______________________________________________

_______________________________________________

_______________________________________________



1

2

## Paper 2: Animal power

**9.** Which of the following statements are true, false or are not possible to know from the file? Tick the appropriate box for each.



| Fact | True | False | Not possible to know from the file |
| --- | --- | --- | --- |
| Toothed and baleen whales fight each other. | | | |
| Humpback whales are the most popular with tourists. | | | |
| All whales are still under threat from hunting. | | | |
| Narwhal whales fight with their tusks. | | | |

2

## Paper 2: Animal power

**10.** Look at the chart on page 6. Why do you think Narwhal tusks were believed to be from unicorns?

Marks

1

**11.** The *Whales fact file* provides a large amount of information in a small amount of space. How does it do this effectively while keeping readers interested? Refer to specific examples in your answer.

Marks

3

## Paper 2: Animal power

Marks

---

Questions 12–16 are about *The Wind in the Willows* extract on pages **7–8** in the Reading Booklet.

**12.** What mood does the opening paragraph establish?

________________________________________

________________________________________

________________________________________

________________________________________

________________________________________

2

---

**13.** Find a quote each for the Mole and the Rat that describes how they are feeling.

● Mole: ___________________________________

________________________________________

________________________________________

● Rat: ____________________________________

________________________________________

________________________________________

2

---

## Paper 2: Animal power

**14.** Badger says: *"At this very moment, perhaps, Toad is busy arraying himself in those singularly hideous habiliments so dear to him, which transform him from a (comparatively) good-looking Toad into an Object which throws any decent-minded animal that comes across it into a violent fit."* (Paragraph 10)

What effect is he trying to have on Ratty and Mole?

_______________________________________________

_______________________________________________

_______________________________________________

_______________________________________________

**Marks**

**2**

**15.** *"Right you are!"* cried the Rat, starting up. *"We'll rescue the poor unhappy animal! We'll convert him! He'll be the most converted Toad that ever was before we've done with him!"* (Paragraph 11)

Why do they want to convert Toad?

_______________________________________________

_______________________________________________

_______________________________________________

**1**

# Paper 2: Animal power

**16.** Describe Badger's character, referring to the text to justify your ideas. Refer to paragraphs 5–10 for your answer.

Marks

3

## Paper 2: Animal power

Question 17 is about all three texts in the Reading Booklet.

Marks

**17.** Imagine you have been asked to bury a time capsule for people hundreds of years in the future, and you must include only one of the three texts in the booklet. Which one would you choose, and why?

3

**End of test**

[BLANK PAGE]

[BLANK PAGE]

[BLANK PAGE]

| Question | Focus | Possible marks | Actual marks |
|---|---|---|---|
| 1 | AF3 | 1 | |
| 2 | AF5 | 3 | |
| 3 | AF6 | 2 | |
| 4 | AF4 | 2 | |
| 5 | AF6 | 1 | |
| 6 | AF2 | 1 | |
| 7 | AF4 | 1 | |
| 8 | AF6 | 2 | |
| 9 | AF3 | 2 | |
| 10 | AF3 | 1 | |
| 11 | AF4 | 3 | |
| 12 | AF6 | 2 | |
| 13 | AF4 | 2 | |
| 14 | AF6 | 2 | |
| 15 | AF3 | 1 | |
| 16 | AF5 | 3 | |
| 17 | AF7 | 3 | |
| **Total** | | **32** | |

Percentage mark = $\dfrac{\text{child score} \times 100}{32}$ = __________ %

# War Children
## Reading Booklet

# Contents




**Acknowledgements**
The publishers gratefully acknowledge permission to reproduce the following copyright material:

Peter Riley for the use of the 'Operation Pied Piper' by Peter Riley. Text © 2013, Peter Riley.
Eileen Jones for the use of the 'Diary of an evacuee' by Eileen Jones. Text © 2013, Eileen Jones.
Jillian Powell for the use of the 'Message in the Rubble' by Jillian Powell. Text © 2013, Jillian Powell.

# Operation Pied Piper

## Background: fearful memories

The memories of the First World War – horrific injuries from gas attacks in trench battles and 1400 dead in air raids on Britain – provided a powerful stimulus to the British government as it responded to the imminent threat of war in the late 1930s. Massive air raids were anticipated that would drop gas and bombs on major cities as the enemy tried to destroy the nation's will to fight. These were anxious times.

## Logistics: planning for safety

Materials for constructing air raid shelters – *Anderson Shelters* – were made available, and gas masks were issued to save people from a choking death that the deadly mustard gas would bring. For city children, an exercise with the code name *Operation Pied Piper* was implemented just before war was declared. Children living in *danger zones* – cities such as London, Birmingham and Glasgow – were to  be moved by train or bus to safer *reception zones* in rural and coastal areas, or by ship to neutral countries such as Canada. The children were to take up lodgings, called *billets*, and the householders were to be paid a small sum of money for their upkeep. The plan intended for the children to stay there until the war was over.

## In practice: away from home

Operation Pied Piper took place during the first three days of September in 1939, when nearly 3,000,000 children were evacuated. Babies went with their mothers, but children aged three to thirteen had to leave their parents behind. Each child carried a gas mask; a suitcase with at least one spare change of clothing; and had a label attached to their coat bearing their name, number and school. Many clung to a cuddly toy. For some children it was the first time that they had ever left home, and it was often left to the teachers who went with them to cheer them up by encouraging them to think of it all as a holiday or a great adventure.

# Paper 3: War Children

When the children arrived at their destination, billeting was a much greater problem than had been anticipated. It was hoped that the children could be easily accommodated – turning up at welcoming homes and being warmly received – but the reality was often much less humane. Billeting officers took children to places such as village halls and invited locals to come and choose. Often children were lined up against a wall or paraded on a stage. "I'll take that one," was a phrase frequently used, and often remembered by the evacuees, many now in their eighties.

It was a lottery. Some children were taken into stately homes and had servants to serve them at meal times, while others in had to sleep in the servants' quarters. Most children lived in more ordinary homes. Many were treated as part of the family and became firm friends with the children there, and carry happy memories of that time to this day. Some were not made welcome: the householders considered them scruffy or badly behaved and sometimes beat them. In some places the local children did not like them either and stole evacuees' possessions, adding further misery to an unhappy and often fearful existence.

## Aftermath: changed lives

The anticipated bombing raids did not begin as soon as war was declared in September 1939, and the gas attacks never occurred. All was quiet in Britain until April of 1940, and many people refer to this initial period as the *phoney war*. With seemingly nothing to fear mothers and their babies were the first to leave their billets. Those who had not been made welcome were the next to go, and homesickness

drove many others to leave and take their chances in the danger zones.

Eventually the phoney war did come to an end and the anticipated horrors of bombing destruction commenced. Evacuation was restarted but not in the large numbers of the original Operation Pied Piper. When the war finally ended over fifty thousand evacuees were returned to the cities. Some were fortunate, and resumed their lives with their families. For 76,000 evacuees, however, there was no home or family to return to and they began their post war lives in their new home, where evacuation, and fate, had sent them.

**Wednesday 4th October 1939**

Dear Diary,

I will never get used to Devon ways! The dialect is hard to comprehend and people mock my London accent. There are no pavements here to walk on and the tracks across the fields are awfully muddy; and all the animals frighten me with their grunting, pecking and pushing. Tonight we had potatoes that had come straight from the field! They were very tasty too.

I hate to be away from Mum – I've never written her letters before! I still write home every week, and I long to tell Mum everything. I always manage to write cheerful letters so that Mum will not be anxious or suspicious. She says that she is envious and wishes she could get away from the grimy city into the countryside, and that fortune has smiled on me! Can 'fortune smiling' involve feeling sad inside?

Time for bed, Margaret

**Thursday 5th October 1939**

Dear Diary,

School was better today. Miss Stokes has put the evacuees on double desks in our own row so we can read to each other, not to her. She must be apprehensive that we will abscond and she evidently doubts her ability to give chase – I overheard her telling Mr Williams that she "will not catch fleas!" I would like to reassure her that she is worrying unnecessarily about me – Mum would not want me to run away even though she misses me so much.

I managed to chant most of my times tables this morning, but I stumbled on my seven times table. Mr Williams is listening tomorrow; I pray he won't carry his cane again.

I was too long scouring the saucepan. I wish I had finished in time for tea.

Yours hungrily, Margaret

## Paper 3: War Children

**Saturday 7th October 1939**

Dearest Diary,

Something marvellous happened today! I was pumping water into the bucket when Mrs Brennan rushed out, all agitated. She told me to hurry in, change from my pinafore, put on my own clothes, brush my hair and come into the front room – where I had never been before. Mum was there! Even Mrs Brennan had not expected her to visit so soon.

Mum and I walked and shared her sandwiches. She clutched my hand and I answered her urgent questions cautiously. She let slip how much she missed me. Was that why she visited so soon? She commented that I looked paler and thinner, but was reassured that I was just growing. Then Mrs Brennan made a banquet of ham, eggs and cakes! I even had a chair, and Mrs Brennan made no mention of dirtying its good cover.

Mum looked lonely and her eyes glistened when she departed. This time I struggled to restrain selfish tears. I certainly did not complain about being cold in bed or having to get water from outside. Only you can know that dear diary.

Your loving friend, Margaret

# Message in the Rubble

by Jillian Powell

Tim's head had scarcely touched the pillow when he heard the familiar nagging whine of the siren.

"Tim, Laura! Dressing gowns and coats on, hurry," Mum called. "Don't forget your gas masks."

The Anderson shelter stood at the bottom of the garden. Its rounded tin roof protruded like a gleaming skull from the banks of turf dad had heaped around it.

"Why did you have to dig ours so deep, Reg?" Mum scolded Dad. "It's like going into your grave."

"You'll be glad of it one day Ethel," Dad had said as he dug out the earth where dahlias had once bloomed. Mum had been adamant: there was no way their children were being evacuated to live with strangers. The shelter must be their protection from Jerry's Dorniers and Heinkels.

Tim and Laura hated the Anderson. It was cold and cramped with narrow bunks squashed against the arc of the corrugated tin walls. From inside, they could hear the menacing drone of the German bombers, and the walls occasionally reverberated with the sound of falling bombs. Tonight they sounded louder than ever. Dad stood with his arms outstretched like a cross, shielding the door of the shelter. "They're miles away," he repeated as Tim and Laura huddled with Mum in the cavernous dark, lit only by a feeble oil lamp. Tim watched gloomy shadows dance and morph on the walls as the dull thud of the bombs got louder and louder, until suddenly there was a deafening crash. The shelter seemed to judder and lift out of the ground. Earth spewed down the steps.

It was getting light when the all-clear sounded. They crawled out of the shelter into a cold dawn. The garden was shrouded in dust and smoke. An acrid smell hung in the air, it reminded Tim of the time they had tried making toffee apples and Mum had burned the saucepan. As rays of morning sun sliced through the murk the family stood staring in silence. Their home had been dissected by a German bomber. It looked like Laura's dolls house with the front taken off. The flowery wallpaper in Mum and Dad's bedroom was blotched with smoke. The wardrobe's door was missing, a crumpled dress hung alone. A row of china cup handles hanging on hooks was all that was left of the pantry.

"Oh, they've taken our home Reg," Mum said, too stunned to cry.

"We are all in one piece, that's the main thing," Dad said, but Tim could hear the choke in his voice.

"Where are we to go?" Mum said. Now she began to cry.

"They'll find us somewhere, don't fret Ethel," Dad said. His eyes were taking in a panorama of desolation. It had been a direct hit and where their neighbours' houses had been were piles of rubble exuding clouds of brick dust that mingled with the smoke from burning fires.

"The Harris' shelter. It's gone!" Mum said.

"What about Mr Harris' pigeons?" Tim said, but he could already see, the pigeon loft had gone too. Shrapnel had demolished everything in its path. Timbers stuck up like bones from piles of debris. An air raid warden was picking his way through. "All survivors must report to the rest centre," he informed them. They stared in mute horror. Tim saw his mum turn her gaze to him and Laura. He knew what she was thinking.

"I want Rosie!" Laura cried. Tim took her hand; finding Laura's most precious possession seemed impossible, but he knew they must try. Carefully, they negotiated the smoking rubble.

"Listen!" Tim said. "Did you hear that, Laura?" He could hear a muffled sound. Tim squatted, the dust making him cough. "It's a pigeon!" He said. The bird was trapped between a timber joist and a pile of bricks. Tim spoke to it gently as he began to move the bricks aside.

"Poor thing," Laura said.

"It's one of Mr Harris'," Tim said. "It must have been heading home." The bird was alive, its eyes blinking, its pulse racing. Tim cupped his hands, carefully lifting it out. "I think it's broken its leg," he said. Then he spotted it: a tiny canister attached to the pigeon's leg. "It's carrying a secret message Laura," Tim said. "We have to take this pigeon to the police station. It's carrying a message from behind enemy lines!"

# READING TEST

## PAPER 3: WAR CHILDREN



| First name | |
|---|---|
| Middle name | |
| Last name | |
| Date of birth | Day     Month     Year |
| Year group | |
| School | |

## REMEMBER

- This paper is **60 minutes** long.
- You have **10 minutes** to read the reading booklets before answering the questions. During this time you should not open your answer booklet.
- You then have **50 minutes** to write your answers in this booklet.
- There are 17 questions totalling 34 marks.

# Paper 3: War Children

Questions 1–6 are about Operation Pied Piper on pages **3–4** in the Reading Booklet.

Marks

**1.** Look at the paragraph 'Background: fearful memories'. What do you think the writer wants to achieve from this opening section?

_______________________________________________

_______________________________________________

_______________________________________________

_______________________________________________

_______________________________________________

2

**2.** Look at how the article has been presented. How has it been organised to make it easy to navigate?

_______________________________________________

_______________________________________________

_______________________________________________

_______________________________________________

1

## Paper 3: War Children

**3.** Which two of these statements are true? Tick the appropriate boxes.

- ☐ Mustard gas was dropped on England.

- ☐ Most children returned home before the war had ended.

- ☐ Some children went with their mothers.

- ☐ Children were allocated to families in advance.

Marks

1

**4.** How does the writer help us to empathise with the evacuated children? Provide at least one example from the text.

_______________________________________

_______________________________________

_______________________________________

_______________________________________

_______________________________________

2

## Paper 3: War Children

**5.** Look at the section on logistics. Explain how the author helps us to understand specific words concerning the operation.

Marks

1

**6.** What does 'billet' mean?

1

## Paper 3: War Children



> Questions 7–10 are about *Diary of an evacuee* on pages **5–6** in the Reading Booklet.

**7.** Look at Margaret's diary entry for Wednesday 4th October 1939. Find a quote that suggests that she feels uneasy in her new home. Explain your choice.

_______________________________________________

_______________________________________________

_______________________________________________

_______________________________________________

_______________________________________________

2

## Paper 3: War Children

**8.** Explain what these quotes tell us about Miss Stokes.



**a)** *Miss Stokes has put the evacuees on double desks in our own row so we can read to each other, not to her.*
(5th October 1939)

Margaret's interpretation: _______________________

_______________________

_______________________

Other possible meaning: _______________________

_______________________

_______________________

**b)** *I overheard her telling Mr Williams that she "will not catch flees!"* (5th October 1939)

Margaret's interpretation: _______________________

_______________________

_______________________

Other possible meaning: _______________________

_______________________

_______________________

2

## Paper 3: War Children

**9.** What does the final entry imply about Mrs Brennan without actually saying anything negative? Explain your answer.



3

# Paper 3: War Children

**10.** Using quotes where necessary, explain what the diary reveals about Margaret's attitudes and personality.

Marks

_______________________________________________

_______________________________________________

_______________________________________________

_______________________________________________

_______________________________________________

_______________________________________________

_______________________________________________

3

Questions 11–16 are about *Message in the Rubble* on pages **7–8** in the Reading Booklet.

**11.** Pick out three words or phrases that help give a feel for the Anderson Shelter. Explain the effect of each one.

**a)** _______________________________

_______________________________

_______________________________

**b)** _______________________________

_______________________________

_______________________________

**c)** _______________________________

_______________________________

_______________________________

3

## Paper 3: War Children

**12.** What sort of person is Tim and Laura's dad? Use quotes to justify your answer.

_______________________________________________

_______________________________________________

_______________________________________________

_______________________________________________

Marks

2

## Paper 3: War Children



**13.** After they leave the shelter the family see that the Harris' shelter is gone. The text then says: *"Tim saw his mum turn her gaze to him and Laura. He knew what she was thinking."*

What do **you** imagine she was thinking?

2

## Paper 3: War Children

**14.** Look at paragraphs 3 and 4, when the family leave the shelter. How does the author make you feel like you are there? Give examples.

Marks

3

**15.** What does "Jerry's Dorniers and Heinkels" mean?
(Paragraph 1)

_______________________________________________

_______________________________________________



1

**16.** Do you think Tim is older or younger than Laura? Explain
your answer.

_______________________________________________

_______________________________________________

_______________________________________________

2

# Paper 3: War Children

Question 17 is about all three texts in the Reading Booklet.



**17.** Which text is the most reliable for learning about what life was really like for evacuees in World War II? Explain why, discussing the strengths and weaknesses of all three texts.

___________________________________________

___________________________________________

___________________________________________

___________________________________________

___________________________________________

___________________________________________

___________________________________________

___________________________________________

___________________________________________

___________________________________________

___________________________________________

___________________________________________

**End of test**

3

[BLANK PAGE]

| Question | Focus | Possible marks | Actual marks |
|---|---|---|---|
| 1 | AF6 | 2 | |
| 2 | AF4 | 1 | |
| 3 | AF2 | 1 | |
| 4 | AF6 | 2 | |
| 5 | AF4 | 1 | |
| 6 | AF2 | 1 | |
| 7 | AF3 | 2 | |
| 8 | AF3 | 2 | |
| 9 | AF4 | 3 | |
| 10 | AF6 | 3 | |
| 11 | AF5 | 3 | |
| 12 | AF3 | 2 | |
| 13 | AF3 | 2 | |
| 14 | AF5 | 3 | |
| 15 | AF3 | 1 | |
| 16 | AF3 | 2 | |
| 17 | AF7 | 3 | |
| **Total** | | **34** | |

Percentage mark = $\dfrac{\text{child score}}{34} \times 100 =$ __________ %

# LEVEL 6
# READING
## National Curriculum Tests

## Guidance and Mark Schemes

Book End, Range Road, Witney, Oxfordshire, OX29 0YD
www.scholastic.co.uk
©2013 Scholastic Ltd
789  56789012

A British Library Cataloguing-in-Publication Data
A catalogue record for this book is available from the
British Library.

ISBN 978-1407-12812-2
Printed and bound by Bell & Bain Ltd, Glasgow







**Author**
Paul Hollin

**Editorial team**
Rachel Morgan, Melissa Rugless

**Design team**
Shelley Best, Andrea Lewis





**Acknowledgements**
Extracts from Department for Education website
© Crown Copyright. Reproduced under the terms of
the Open Government Licence (OGL). http://www.
nationalarchives.gov.uk/doc/open-government-
licence/open-government-licence.htm

Images for the Reading Booklet:
© Maisna/Shutterstock.com; © rusty elliott/Photos.
com; © Atlaspix/Shutterstock.com; © Photos.com;
© idreamphoto/Shutterstock.com; © istockphoto.com/
Corey Ford; © iStockphoto.com/Oliver Childs;
© iStockphoto.com/Arthur Kwiatkowski; © Jim
Tierney/Photos.com; © Trinity Mirror/Mirrorpix/Alamy

Every effort has been made to trace copyright
holders for the works reproduced in this publication,
and the publishers apologise or any inadvertent
omissions.

# Guidance and Mark Schemes for Reading: Level 6

| Contents | Page |
|---|---|

## About this pack

This pack provides you with practice papers to help support children with the Level 6 Reading test and assess whether they are suitable to be entered for it. The pack consists of this introductory booklet and three sample papers covering a wide-range of Level 6 content taken from the upper end of Key Stage 2 and the Key Stage 3 programme of study.

## Deciding on children's suitability

To take the Level 6 test, children should be working very securely at Level 5 from early in their final year of Key Stage 2, and they should be accessing the Key Stage 3 curriculum for several months prior to the tests. To achieve a Level 6 the children need to score around 55% to 70%, depending on the particular paper. As a rough guide, when using these sample papers it is suggested that children consistently scoring under 50% are probably not ready.

Below are the National Curriculum Attainment Targets for Levels 5 and 6 for Reading. Looking at these carefully you can see the progression of skills and understanding through the levels, in particular the degree of child articulation required. Level 6 requires that children give lucid responses that show a strong awareness as to whether their test answers are thorough and coherent.

### Level 5

*Pupils show understanding of a range of texts, selecting essential points and using inference and deduction where appropriate. In their responses, they identify key features, themes and characters and select sentences, phrases and relevant information to support their views. They understand that texts fit into historical and literary traditions. They retrieve and collate information from a range of sources.*

### Level 6

*In reading and discussing a range of texts, pupils identify different layers of meaning and comment on their significance and effect. They give personal responses to literary texts, referring to aspects of language, structure and themes in justifying their views, and making connections between texts from different times and cultures and their own experiences. They summarise a range of information from different sources.*

### Level 6 checklist

The Reading paper uses Assessment Focuses (AFs) to categorise questions. For each of these areas a strong degree of competence in demonstrating and explaining understanding is needed, as reflected in the Attainment Target for Level 6 Reading (see above).

The seven AFs represent a development of reader cognition and as such AF1 is not explicitly tested in the papers and AF2 receives scant attention. Similarly, due to the complexity of this focus, AF7 accounts for a small percentage of marks.

# Reading Assessment Focuses

**AF1 Use a range of strategies, including accurate decoding of text, to read for meaning.**
*Not explicitly tested.*

**AF2 Understand, describe, select or retrieve information, events or ideas from texts and use quotation and reference to text.**
*Can children quickly find relevant information in texts, explaining their choices using quotes or by paraphrasing?*

**AF3 Deduce, infer or interpret information, events or ideas from texts**
*Can children use inferential skills to understand and interpret texts then explain their choices? Can they answer open ended questions with well-rounded, lucid answers?*

**AF4 Identify and comment on the structure and organisation of texts, including grammatical and presentational features at text level.**
*Can children explain rationale and stylistic choices that contribute to the overall shape and structure of what they are reading? Ideally this should be done with reference to specific grammatical terms, such as passive voice or figurative language.*

**AF5 Explain and comment on writers' uses of language, including grammatical and literary features at word and sentence level.**
*Can children explain why particular sections of text are effective and what they mean?*

**AF6 Identify and comment on writers' purposes and viewpoints, and the overall effect of the text on the reader.**
*Can children appreciate author motivation and viewpoint and how this can affect different readers?*

**AF7 Relate texts to their social, cultural and historical contexts and literary traditions.**
*Can children demonstrate an understanding of the text within a broader context? They should be able to demonstrate awareness of the characteristics of text genres and the factors influencing its creation and style.*

## The Level 6 assessment tests

There is a single reading paper that contains questions totalling 30–35 marks, with 1 hour allowed (10 minutes reading and 50 minutes to answer the questions).

## Using the practice papers

The practice papers in this pack can be used as you would any other practice materials. The children will need to be familiar with specific test-focused skills, such as reading carefully, leaving questions if they seem too difficult, working at a suitable pace, and of course checking through their work.

If you choose to use the papers for looking at content rather than practising tests do be aware of the time factor. The tests require a lot of work to be done in 1 hour as they are testing the degree of competence children have – it is not enough to be able to answer questions correctly but slowly.

## Marking and assessing the papers

The mark schemes and answers are located in the latter half of this booklet.

Marking is tricky: answers in literacy will be varied and subjective from child to child, and a fair degree of marker discretion and interpretation is needed, particularly if children's understanding and skills have to be deduced from their answers. The mark schemes provided, detail examples of correct answers (although other variations/phrasings are often acceptable) and an explanation about what the answer should contain to be awarded a mark or marks.

As mentioned earlier, the thresholds for Level 6 vary each year according to difficulty levels. For the sample tests in this pack, as a basic guideline it is suggested that pupils consistently obtaining less than 50–60% are probably not ready to sit the Level 6 tests.

## Teaching reading to Level 6

Ideally, children who are being considered to be entered for the Level 6 test should receive focused individual or group support at least once a week. Some schools might achieve this by freeing up teacher time, providing a confident Teaching Assistant or parent helper, or even forging links with their local Secondary school – either to provide resources or to offer suitable one-off lessons.

In planning for Level 6 work in your classroom, three useful things to bear in mind are:

- All of the knowledge and skills needed to achieve Level 6 build on the knowledge and skills obtained at Level 5.

- Children working at this high a level usually have reasonable degrees of autonomy and self-study skills. Providing them with the appropriate checklists can help them to monitor their own performance as well as work together on problems.

- The main emphasis for developing children's skills at Level 6 should focus on both the inference of meaning coupled with a clear understanding of how the writer achieves their aims, both in terms of their organisation of language and the stylistic and literary features employed: in other words, identifying and understanding the craft and intentions of the writer.

# Mark Scheme for Paper 1: *Anne of Green Gables*

| Q | Answers | Mark | AF |
|---|---|---|---|
| 1 | **Award 3 marks** for answers that identify Anne as the lead character, explain why specific words have been used **and** explore their implications for Anne's personality or state of mind.<br>For example: *The author is trying to show us the sort of person Anne is: "Reverie", "dreamy" and "wondering afar" suggest that she is maybe a daydreamer, and the words "soul" and "star-led" suggest that there may also be something deep or mysterious about Anne.*<br><br>**Award 2 marks** for answers that indicate an awareness of portraying Anne's personality or state of mind **and** suggest what that might be.<br>For example: *The author is trying to tell us that Anne is a thoughtful and imaginative person.*<br><br>**Award 1 mark** for answers that indicate an awareness of portraying Anne's personality or state of mind.<br>For example: *The author is trying to give an impression about Anne's personality.* | Up to 3 | AF5 |
| 2 | **Award 1 mark** for either (including reference to the text):<br>● she lived in an asylum (*There was a girl at the asylum...*)<br>● she has never had a proper home (*I've never had a real home since I can remember*). | 1 | AF2 |
| 3 | **Award 1 mark** for any quote that suggests her optimism such as:<br>● *Something still pleasanter may come after...*<br>● *It gives me that pleasant ache again just to think of coming to a really truly home.*<br>● *It's the first thing I ever saw that couldn't be improved upon by imagination.*<br><br>**Award no marks** for a quote that points towards the beauty of things, such as:<br>● *"Pretty? Oh, PRETTY doesn't seem the right word to use. Nor beautiful, either."* | 1 | AF3 |
| 4 | **Award 2 marks** for answers that suggest how the long meandering statement of Anne reveals excitement.<br>For example: *Anne talks a lot, repeating certain words with emphasis, and says whatever is on her mind. "Pretty? Oh, PRETTY doesn't seem the right word to use." She seems to have butterflies in her tummy because she has a "queer ache".*<br><br>**Award 1 mark** for an appropriate quote from Anne.<br>For example: *Anne says "Oh, it was wonderful—wonderful. It's the first thing I ever saw that couldn't be improved upon by imagination."* | Up to 2 | AF5 |

| Q | Answers | Mark | AF |
|---|---------|------|-----|
| **5** | **Award 2 marks** for words and quotes that identify the excitable and romantic nature of Anne. For example:<br>● *"It just satisfies me here"—she put one hand on her breast—"it made a queer funny ache and yet it was a pleasant ache."*<br>● *I know because of the thrill. When I hit on a name that suits exactly it gives me a thrill.*<br><br>**And** the serious and down-to-earth nature of Matthew. Such as:<br>● *"Well now, you must mean the Avenue," said Matthew after a few moments' profound reflection. "It is a kind of pretty place."*<br>● *"It always kind of gives me a thrill to see them ugly white grubs that spade up in the cucumber beds. I hate the look of them."*<br><br>**Award 1 mark** at your discretion if only the words or the quotes are suitable. | Up to 2 | AF3 |
| **6** | **Award 3 marks** for quotes **and** explanations of the metaphorical content.<br>For example: *The author wants to make us feel the way Anne did when she first saw the scene. Phrases like "the most spiritual shadings of crocus and rose" make it seem sacred, and "a white-clad girl tip-toeing to her own reflection" make it feel alive.*<br><br>**Award 2 marks** for pointing to the detailed adjectives.<br>For example: *The author uses describing words like amber-hued belt of sand-hills, the dark blue gulf, and ethereal green to make the colours seem different to how we usually imagine them.*<br><br>**Award 1 mark** for more general answers stating that the description is about impressions rather than a practical account.<br>For example: *The author gives the reader an impression of the different colours and shades, rather than an accurate and literal description of the location.*<br><br>**Award no marks** for answers that only state that the author tells us what is there. | Up to 3 | AF5 |
| **7** | **Award 2 marks** for answers that notice how the openings offer appealing things **and** quote specific words to show this.<br>For example: *Words like paradise, appetite, and a warm welcome are all nice things. They make us think something good will be revealed, and we want to know what it is.*<br><br>**Award 1 mark** for stating that they are all positive in tone.<br>For example: *They are all positive statements. They create a good feeling about the island.* | Up to 2 | AF4 |



**SCHOLASTIC** Guidance and Mark Schemes

| Q | Answers | Mark | AF |
|---|---|---|---|
| 8 | **Award I mark** for any two of these quotes:<br>• *considered a paradise by visitors*<br>• *renowned fresh shellfish*<br>• *one of the many hire shops*<br><br>(Note that these all imply popularity.) | I | AF2 |
| 9 | **Award 2 marks** for specific references to events, people and places that might link the author to Anne.<br>For example: *The brochure tells us that she grew up on Prince Edward Island and in the same period that the book is set. As a child, she also regularly visited family at their "green-gabled farmhouse" and her life was similar to an orphan's because she wasn't raised by her mother and father.*<br><br>**Award I mark** for answers that only point to the farmhouse that inspired her.<br>For example: *It says that the setting for* Anne of Green Gables *"was inspired by the green-gabled farmhouse that Maud often visited as a child".* | Up to 2 | AF3 |
| 10 | **Award 2 marks** for answers that show an appreciation of the language that implies a real place.<br>For example: *The brochure uses words that make it seem real. Words like "look around" and "chat" suggest that we will be involved, and "Marilla's spotless pantry" sounds like it is real.*<br><br>**Award I mark** for pointing out that the characters and locations are described in detail.<br>For example: *It describes the characters and locations in detail, using names from the book.* | Up to 2 | AF5 |
| 11 | Answers may be positive or negative.<br><br>**Award 2 marks** for answers that point to layout, variety, and language used (positively or negatively), with justifications.<br>For example: *I thought that it tried too hard to persuade us to like the island. There was too much text about the LM Montgomery, and not enough about the rest of the island. Also, I think the text should be split up under more subheadings to make it easier to read.*<br><br>**Award I mark** for answers that show an awareness of structure **and** note specific aspects in a relevant way.<br>For example: *I liked the brochure because it has something for everyone, and different sections were presented in different styles, which keeps you interested.* | Up to 2 | AF4 |
| 12 | **Award I mark** for a tick next to FamilyMorris – all of the other points have opinion in them. | I | AF2 |

| Q | Answers | Mark | AF |
|---|---|---|---|
| 13 | **Award 1 mark** for any two of *gross, awash, enchanting* or *engulfs*. | 1 | AF3 |
| 14 | **Award 2 marks** for answers that suggest viewpoints based on two specific quotes.<br>For example: *"We will certainly return!" suggests that familyMorris loves the island and all the tourist facilities; they don't seem to mind anything, even the rain. shannon61 is less keen though, saying that "it weakens LM Montgomery's legacy".*<br><br>**Award 1 mark** for answers which identify two views **or** if one detailed view is given with an accompanying quote.<br>For example: *shannon61 likes the island but thinks tourism is spoiling it, but familyMorris love it.*<br><br>**Award no marks** if only one simple view is provided. | Up to 2 | AF6 |
| 15 | **Award 2 marks** for answers that notice how the entry states facts and concludes with a clear statement.<br>For example: *He states facts: he is an islander so tourism is very important for him and the island, and although he admits it is "tacky" he ends by saying he has to make a living.*<br><br>**Award 1 mark** for suggesting that he makes it clear that he is an islander so he should be taken seriously.<br>For example: *He explains that he and his friends are affected by the tourism because they live there, so his opinion matters.* | Up to 2 | AF4 |
| 16 | **Award 2 marks** for answers that explore the benefit of a written record for all versus the limitation of shorter answers that can be one-sided.<br>For example: *It would be helpful because you can read comments whenever you want and show them to other people, and there are different points of view. The problem is that I don't know the people and so I don't know if I can trust their views or not.*<br><br>**Award 1 mark** for expressing a preference either way with some degree of logical justification.<br>For example: *I would rather talk to someone I know who has been there so I could ask my own questions.* | Up to 2 | AF7 |



**SCHOLASTIC** Guidance and Mark Schemes

| Q | Answers | Mark | AF |
|---|---------|------|-----|
| 17 | **Award 3 marks** for answers that explore and contrast the figurative language of the extract with the promotional style of the brochure, noting examples.<br>For example: *The brochure is trying to persuade us that it is a good place to go on holiday where we will enjoy ourselves. It talks about "famous red sandy beaches". But the extract is a story that uses imagery to help the reader visualise the setting effectively. For example, the descriptions are very detailed, such as the "amber-hued belt of sand-hills".*<br><br>**Award 2 marks** for answers that clearly acknowledge the two styles but with limited examples or reference.<br>For example: *The extract is trying to describe a new scene that we have never seen before, but the brochure is trying to make it seem as nice as possible for a holiday. The brochure also has to be shorter as people don't look for long.*<br><br>**Award 1 mark** for accurately explaining the difference between the two styles.<br>For example: *The brochure is factual and wants to encourage us to go to the island. It also has pictures to help it. The extract is much more romantic.* | Up to 3 | AF7 |

# Mark Scheme for Paper 2: *Animal Power*

| Q | Answers | Mark | AF |
|---|---|---|---|
| 1 | **Award 1 mark** for any answer that includes the word immortal. | 1 | AF3 |
| 2 | **Award 3 marks** for answers that discuss the quote in detail, explaining the metaphor.<br>For example: *The noise and heat of the blacksmith's workshop is fascinating but scary. It make you think about something being created that has lots of energy and power, something you should be cautious of because it is so powerful.*<br><br>**Award 2 marks** for answers that clearly acknowledge the metaphor but with limited reference.<br>For example: *They are good metaphors the poem is wondering about how the tyger was made, and the blacksmith's tools and furnace are used to make things.*<br><br>**Award 1 mark** for making the link between creation.<br>For example: *It makes you think about something being created.* | Up to 3 | AF5 |
| 3 | **Award 2 marks** for answers that offer a rounded view on the poet's thoughts.<br>For example: *The poet is trying to show that he cannot understand how such an animal exists, and he is asking God why.*<br><br>**Award 1 mark** for a sensible idea of the poet's opinion.<br>For example: *To show that he is confused.*<br><br>**Award no marks** for answers that do not focus on the poet.<br>For example: *To make us think.* | Up to 2 | AF6 |
| 4 | **Award 2 marks** for answers that comment on the symmetry and/or that the poet has not found any answers.<br>For example: *It brings the poem round in a circle, drawing the reader back to the original question and shows that he still doesn't know the answer. The only progression is that poet changes could to dare, which makes him seem more scared, because he has realised how powerful the tiger is.*<br><br>**Award 1 mark** for any one of the above points.<br><br>**Award no marks** for answers that do not include one of these points. | Up to 2 | AF4 |
| 5 | **Award 1 mark** for answers that note the encouraging and positive tone of the introduction to set the reader in an interested frame of mind. | 1 | AF6 |



**SCHOLASTIC** Guidance and Mark Schemes

| Q | Answers | Mark | AF |
|---|---|---|---|
| 6 | **Award 1 mark** only if both facts are correct, chosen from:<br>*Toothed whales outnumber baleens in species; their teeth are for grabbing and chewing prey, attack and defence, or exhibiting dominance.*<br>*Baleen whales are usually superior in size; they have two blowholes; they have a baleen palate instead of teeth; they filter feed.*<br><br>**Award no marks** for other facts (for example: migration; pods) that are not unequivocal in the brochure. | 1 | AF2 |
| 7 | **Award 1 mark** for answers that clearly identify that diet and habitat are linked/interconnected. | 1 | AF4 |
| 8 | **Award 2 marks** for answers that comment on the variation of content and facts.<br>For example: *The chart has lots of different little facts in it. Some are just about the whales' features, but others are unusual, like their nicknames. You want to keep reading because you don't know what sort of information will come next.*<br><br>**Award 1 mark** for answers that point out the variety of information.<br>For example: *There is lots of different information about each whale that helps you to imagine what they are like.*<br><br>**Award no marks** for answers that simply state that the chart presents information clearly. | Up to 2 | AF6 |
| 9 | **Award 2 marks** for all answers correct.<br><br>**Award 1 mark** for two or three answers correct. | Up to 2 | AF3 |

| Fact | True | False | Not possible to know from the file? |
|---|---|---|---|
| Toothed and baleen whales fight each other | | | ✔ |
| Humpback whales are the most popular with tourists. | | ✔ | |
| All whales are still under threat from hunting. | | | ✔ |
| Narwhal whales fight with their tusks. | ✔ | | |

| Q | Answers | Mark | AF |
|---|---|---|---|
| 10 | **Award 1 mark** for answers that correctly identify either of the following points:<br>● *The chart says that their tusks are "used as a jousting weapon" so it must be long and straight in shape, like a unicorn's horn.*<br>● *In medieval times people were very superstitious and did not know much about whales.*<br><br>**Award no marks** for answers that only state that the tusk looked like a unicorn's horn. | I | AF3 |
| 11 | **Award 3 marks** for answers that consider the brochure in detail, listing specific features.<br>For example: *The brochure arranges the information clearly and in a good order, giving a general introduction then presenting each section with a subheading. It highlights important keywords and uses tables of information in short sentences that are easier to read. It also uses a simple chart to provide facts about different types of whale, which readers can use for interest or reference.*<br><br>**Award 2 marks** for answers that show an awareness of the style of presentation.<br>For example: *It breaks up the information into small chunks to keep you interested. This makes it easy to look at it lots of times without getting confused.*<br><br>**Award 1 mark** for answers that note the variation in presentation.<br>For example: *The brochure has a mixture of charts and sections with titles.* | Up to 3 | AF4 |
| 12 | **Award 2 marks** for answers that indicate the mood with justification.<br>For example: *It creates a happy and positive mood – the start of a warm summer's day that they are excited about.*<br><br>**Award 1 mark** for answers that note the mood.<br>For example: *It creates a bright and busy feel.* | Up to 2 | AF6 |
| 13 | **Award one mark** each for a suitable quote for Rat and Mole, such as:<br>● *"What hour?" asked the Rat uneasily.*<br>● *"Toad's hour, of course!" cried the Mole delightedly.* | Up to 2 | AF4 |



**SCHOLASTIC** Guidance and Mark Schemes

| Q | Answers | Mark | AF |
|---|---|---|---|
| 14 | **Award 2 marks** for answers that clarify Badger's choice of words. For example: *He is trying to persuade them that Toad is making a mistake by putting on an outfit that will not suit him, and that they should be worried about it.*<br><br>**Award 1 mark** for answers that suggest Badger is trying to instigate feelings in Rat and Mole.<br>For example: *He is trying to make them alarmed and anxious about Toad.* | Up to 2 | AF6 |
| 15 | **Award 1 mark** for answers that suggest that Toad is making a mistake **or** that he is a danger to himself and/or others. | 1 | AF3 |
| 16 | **Award 3 marks** for answers that examine Badger's character using quotes/words to justify their views.<br>For example: *Badger seems rather bossy – he says "You two animals will accompany me instantly to Toad Hall" – but he is also the leader. He is confident and sticks to his word – he says "I said I would take him in hand as soon as the winter was well over, and I'm going to take him in hand to-day!" He is very intelligent, using complicated words like "hideous habiliments".*<br><br>**Award 2 marks** for answers that show an understanding of his character with reference to incidents.<br>For example: *He is a rather scary character and is in control of all the others. Ratty and Mole do what he tells them to do, changing their plans as soon as he says so, and he orders the chauffeur to put the car away.*<br><br>**Award 1 mark** for answers that correctly identify key traits with some reference to the text.<br>For example: *Badger is stern, bossy and intelligent. Everyone except Toad is scared of him.*<br><br>**Award no marks** for answers that have no justification from the text. | Up to 3 | AF5 |
| 17 | **Award 3 marks** for answers that clearly justify a choice of text with logical explanations for its value to others. In addition, its merit over the other two texts should be explored and clearly argued.<br><br>**Award 2 marks** for answers that clearly identify the merits of a particular text and why it would be of interest to others.<br><br>**Award 1 mark** for responses that identify a text and appropriately state its merits.<br><br>**Award no marks** for answers that only state a text and provide superficial justifications. | Up to 3 | AF7 |

# Mark Scheme for Paper 3: *War Children*

| Q | Answers | Mark | AF |
|---|---|---|---|
| 1 | **Award 2 marks** for answers that explain the author motivation with reasons.<br>For example: *The author wants us to understand what was in people's minds at the time – the First World War was still a recent memory.*<br><br>**Award 1 mark** for answers correctly identify author intentions.<br>For example: *The author wants us to appreciate the fear people had at the time.*<br><br>**Award no marks** for answers that simply state the author is setting the scene. | Up to 2 | AF6 |
| 2 | **Award 1 mark** for answers that identify that the order of the sections are logically arranged, and/or that the subheadings show us the order. | 1 | AF4 |
| 3 | **Award 1 mark** only if both are correct.<br>• Most children returned home before the war had ended.<br>• Some children went with their mothers. | 1 | AF2 |
| 4 | **Award 2 marks** for answers that identify author intentions with an example.<br>For example: *The author includes details that suggest it was very difficult for the children, such as "children aged three to thirteen had to leave their parents behind".*<br><br>**Award 1 mark** for answers that identify a suitable quote.<br>For example: *The author tells us how the children might be feeling, such as "Many clung to a cuddly toy."*<br><br>**Award no marks** for answers that do not have reference to the text. | Up to 2 | AF6 |
| 5 | **Award 1 mark** for answers that identify the use of italics for specific terms. | 1 | AF4 |
| 6 | **Award 1 mark** for the correct definition of billet – lodgings – even if wording is different from text. | 1 | AF2 |



■SCHOLASTIC  Guidance and Mark Schemes

| Q | Answers | Mark | AF |
|---|---|---|---|
| **7** | **Award 2 marks** for answers that identify a quote relating to the surroundings, with clear justification.<br>For example: *Margaret says "The dialect is hard to comprehend and people mock my London accent", which suggests that she is feeling uneasy – she can't understand what people are saying an they are making fun of her.*<br><br>**Award 1 mark** for answers that identify a quote focusing on Margaret's feelings.<br>For example: *"I hate to be away from mum." This tells us she is missing her mum.* | Up to 2 | AF3 |
| **8** | **Award 1 mark** for each part with two correct responses.<br>**a)** Margaret's interpretations – *Miss Stokes has been considerate to the evacuees.*<br>Other possible meaning – *Miss Stokes wants to keep the evacuees away from the local children and herself.*<br><br>**b)** Margaret's interpretations – *Miss Stokes thinks they will try to run away.*<br>Other possible meaning – *Miss Stokes thinks they are dirty and have fleas on them.* | Up to 2 | AF3 |
| **9** | **Award 3 marks** for answers that identify several references that reveal different aspects of Mrs Brennan, accompanied by an explanation.<br>For example: *Mrs Brennan sounds very mean and selfish. She treats Margaret like a slave! She makes Margaret work very hard doing chores and complains about Margaret getting things dirty, and she doesn't feed Margaret very much.*<br><br>**Award 2 marks** for answers with limited explanation.<br>For example: *Mrs Brennan is very selfish. She makes Margaret do lots of work and gives her very little in return. It looks like she was embarrassed when Margaret's mum arrived.*<br><br>**Award 1 mark** for responses that offer a brief summary of her personality.<br>For example: *Mrs Brennan is very selfish. It sounds like she only had an evacuee to help with all her work.* | Up to 3 | AF4 |

| Q | Answers | Mark | AF |
|---|---------|------|-----|
| 10 | **Award 3 marks** for answers that explore her personality in some depth, with justifications from the text.<br>For example: *Margaret is a thoughtful and honest girl, but maybe a bit too timid as well. She does whatever Mrs Brennan and her teachers tell her to do, and is always thinking about how her mum is feeling. She doesn't complain about how hard life is, and doesn't tell her mum things that would only upset her more. She says "I always manage to write cheerful letters so that Mum will not be anxious or suspicious."*<br><br>**Award 2 marks** for answers with limited explanation.<br>For example: *Margaret is probably tougher than those around her realise. She puts up with scary teachers at school and doing all the work at Mrs Brennan's house because she doesn't want her mum to be worried. She thinks she can't tell anyone except her diary.*<br><br>**Award 1 mark** for answers that comment briefly on her actions.<br>For example: *Although she is having a very hard time Margaret is more worried about her mum than herself. When her mum visits Margaret does not complain about being cold in bed.* | Up to 3 | AF6 |
| 11 | **Award 1 mark** for each correct word or phrase that is accompanied by an appropriate explanation.<br>For example:<br>● *"Cavernous" – makes it seem like a dark cave.*<br>● *"Cramped" – makes it feel small.*<br>● *"It's like going into your grave" – it gives an image of death and darkness.*<br>● *"Its rounded tin roof protruded like a gleaming skull" – a scary place that you don't want to enter.*<br><br>**Award no marks** for words or quotes that simply mention material properties, such as *corrugated*. | Up to 3 | AF5 |

| Q | Answers | Mark | AF |
|---|---|---|---|
| **12** | **Award 2 marks** for two or more responses that identify two or more quotes **and** accurately interpret them.<br>For example:<br>• *Practical and sensible – he has dug a deep and secure Anderson Shelter.*<br>• *He is protective of his family – "Dad stood, with his arms outstretched like a cross, at the door of the shelter."*<br>• *He is positive, he looks on the bright side – "We are all in one piece, that's the main thing..."*<br><br>**Award 1 mark** for one accurate observation of Dad. | Up to 2 | AF3 |
| **13** | **Award 2 marks** for clear answers that are plausible, with a justification.<br>For example: *She was probably thinking that it could just have easily been them. Turning her gaze from where the Harris' shelter had been to her children made him think this.*<br>**Or:** *"She was thinking about the similarities between them – families with children, sitting in an Anderson shelter – and the short distance between their shelters."*<br><br>**Award 1 mark** for answers that are plausible.<br>For example: *She was thinking that an Anderson Shelter won't protect you if a bomb lands right on one.* | Up to 2 | AF3 |
| **14** | **Award 3 marks** for answers that pick out key literary aspects and explain it.<br>For example: *The author uses lots of language to describe the scene and how it feels and smells – "it reminded Tim of the time they had tried making toffee apples and Mum had burned the saucepan" puts a smell of burnt sugar in your mind. After that the strangeness of the smashed house is explained by comparing it to a doll's house. The amount of devastation is revealed slowly, as the characters are taking it all in.*<br><br>**Award 2 marks** for answers that point out more obvious features and explain them.<br>For example: *The text says "The wardrobe's door was missing" and "A row of china cup handles hanging on hooks was all that was left of the pantry". Even if we weren't in the war we can imagine these broken objects.*<br><br>**Award 1 mark** for correctly noting the descriptive style of the text.<br>For example: *The author helps us feel what it was like by using descriptive words like "cold", "shrouded", "acrid" and "murk".* | Up to 3 | AF5 |

| Q | Answers | Mark | AF |
|---|---|---|---|
| 15 | **Award 1 mark** for answers that indicate German planes or German bombs, or enemy planes or bombs.<br><br>**Award no marks** for just planes or bombs. | 1 | AF3 |
| 16 | **Award 2 marks** for answers using examples with justification. For example: *Tim is older than Laura. He looks after her – "Tim took her hand" – and then takes control of the situation when he finds her doll and rescues the pigeon.*<br><br>**Award 1 mark** for answers with less information. For example: *Tim is probably older than Laura because he takes charge.*<br><br>**Award no marks** for answers that do not justify the view. | Up to 2 | AF3 |
| 17 | **Award 3 marks** for answers that clearly justify a choice of text with logical explanations for its benefit to others. In addition, its merit over the other two texts should be explored and a clear argument presented.<br><br>**Award 2 marks** for answers that clearly identify the merits of a particular text and why it would help readers to understand life for children.<br><br>**Award 1 mark** for responses that identify a text and appropriately state its strengths and weaknesses.<br><br>**Award no marks** for answers that only provide superficial justifications. | Up to 3 | AF7 |

# Notes

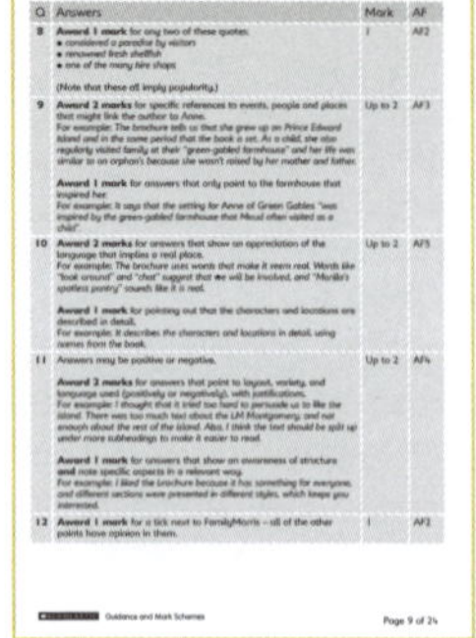

# SCHOLASTIC

## Practice Papers for the National Tests

# Reading Level 6

### Anne of Green Gables

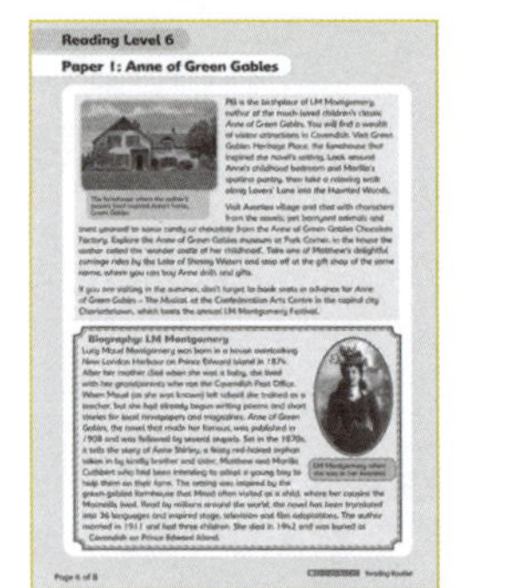

**Reading booklet**

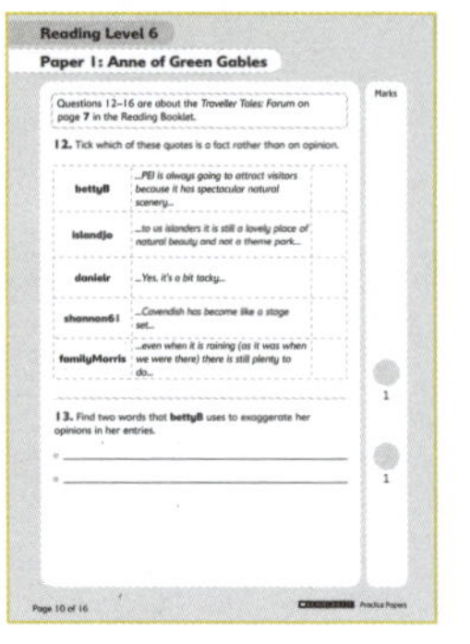

**Test paper**

### Animal Power

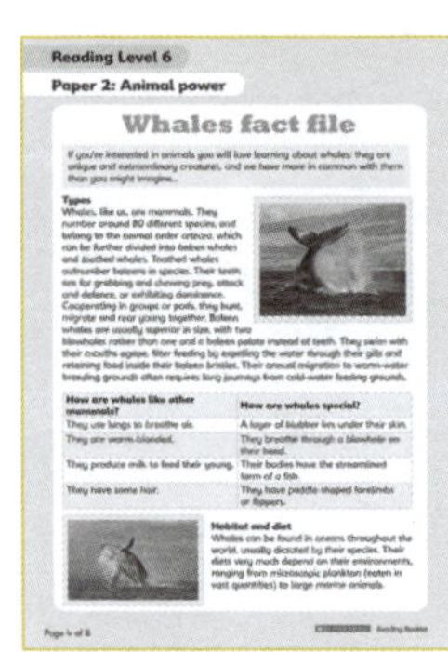

**Reading booklet**

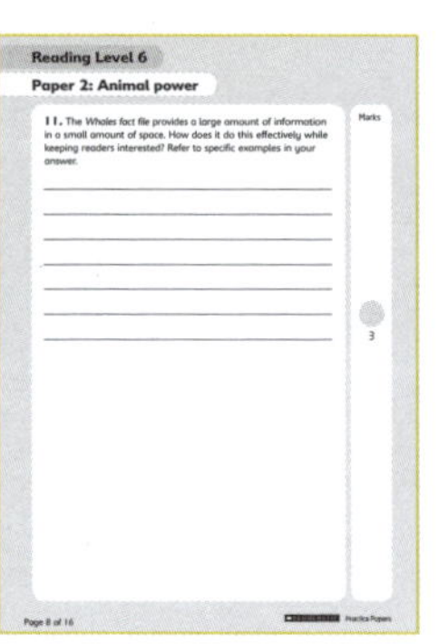

**Test paper**

### War Children

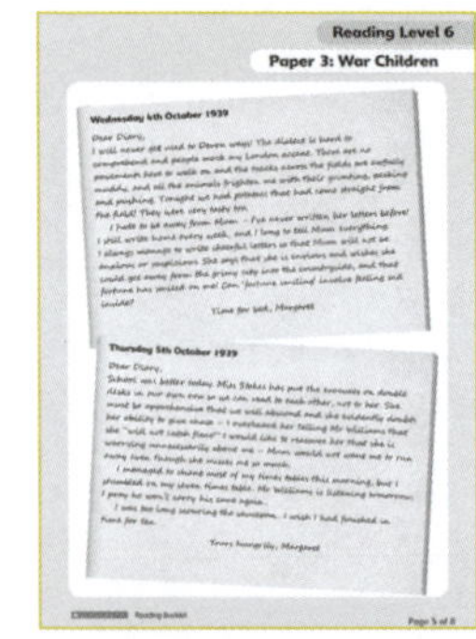

**Reading booklet**

**Test paper**

## 100% in line with the National Tests!

 **Prepare with confidence for the National Tests (SATs)**
These tests are the most authentic practice papers available for the Level 6 Reading Test

 **All the support you need!**
Each test comes with a full mark scheme and clear guidance so you can check your progress

 **Great value for money!**
In this pack you get three complete tests, including full-colour reading booklets, detailed answers, additional support and guidance

### Guidance and Mark Schemes

**Look out for the other great 'Practice Papers'**

**Grammar, Punctuation and Spelling Levels 3–5**
ISBN 978-1407-12810-8

**Grammar, Punctuation and Spelling Level 6**
ISBN 978-1407-12811-5

**Maths Level 6**
ISBN 978-1407-12813-9

Practice Papers for
Reading Level 6

£7.99

**SCHOLASTIC**

ISBN 978-1-407-12812-2

www.scholastic.co.uk